Indian Mary and her youngest daughter, Lillian. This picture was taken about 1902 after Mary moved to Grants Pass from Rogue Canyon country and became active in Salvation Army work. The story of her life has become a legend — the final pages of a last frontier.

THE
LEGEND OF INDIAN MARY
AND UMPQUA JOE

by
PERCY T. BOOTH
Author of
Valley of the Rogues,
Grants Pass, The Golden Years
and
Until The Last Arrow.

Originally Published by
JOSEPHINE COUNTY HISTORICAL SOCIETY
Grants Pass, Oregon

1994, Reprinted by

B & B Publishing
2069 Seventh Street
Coos Bay, Oregon 97420
(503) 269-9277

Dear Readers Of Pioneer History:

B&B Publishing is proud to re-publish this exciting book by Percy T. Booth, that has been out of print for more than 20 years, and once again visit the deep canyons of the Rogue River in one of the West's last frontiers.

We are sure the faded memories recalled by this tale of a good and simple people in a land of hardships will walk with you down a heritage trail, hand in hand with those early trailblazers who opened a wild country of beauty and abundance — the Rogue Valley.

The Legend Of Indian Mary and Umpqua Joe, was the second book about the Rogue Indians written by my late father, following the huge success of his first book, **Valley Of The Rogues**.

One can almost smell the gun powder, hear the rifle shots echoing across the river, see the cabin, and old ferry operated by Indian Mary — but, that is a story best told by Percy T. Booth, author and historian of Grants Pass.

If you enjoy this book, watch for **Until The Last Arrow**, by Percy T. Booth, now being published by Northwest Publishing in Salt Lake City, Utah. The 700 page volume is the first complete chronicles of the rough and tumble times of the early 1800's and the Indian wars of Southern Oregon.

Valley Of The Rogues, and **The Legend Of Indian Mary and Umpqua Joe**, are available in most local book stores, or from B&B Publishing, 2069 7th St., Coos Bay, OR 97420. Enclose $6.95 for **Valley Of The Rogues**, or $7.95 for **The Legend Of Indian Mary and Umpqua Joe**, plus $ 1.50 for postage. Orders of 6 or more books are mailed postpaid.

Richard A. Booth
B&B Publishing

Cover painting by Richard Booth

Percy T. Booth

Introduction

Indian Mary, is a name familiar to residents of Josephine County and the thousands of vacationists who annually enjoy the pleasures of Indian Mary Park, in the Hells Gate Canyon of Rogue River.

But beyond that, what is the true story of her life? Why has she been remembered for more than a century, when such great leaders of the Rogue Tribe as Chief Jo and Chief John, have faded from memory?

And who was Umpqua Joe? Was he really an Umpqua? What series of events made his name a part of the Indian history of a tribe other than his own?

Every early day community proudly claimed its share of pioneer leaders, its trailblazers, and its honored citizens.

But Indian Mary and Umpqua Joe fitted none of these categories. On the contrary, their lives were filled with great sorrow and tragedy. They were simple Indian people, who asked for nothing and received little. But fate, in a series of strange circumstances beyond their control, thrust a degree of legendary significance upon them.

Now, for the first time, after the passage of many years, the answers to these and other questions have been knitted together from a faded yarn of many sources.

I think you will enjoy the true, human story of Indian Mary and Umpqua Joe.

Percy T. Booth

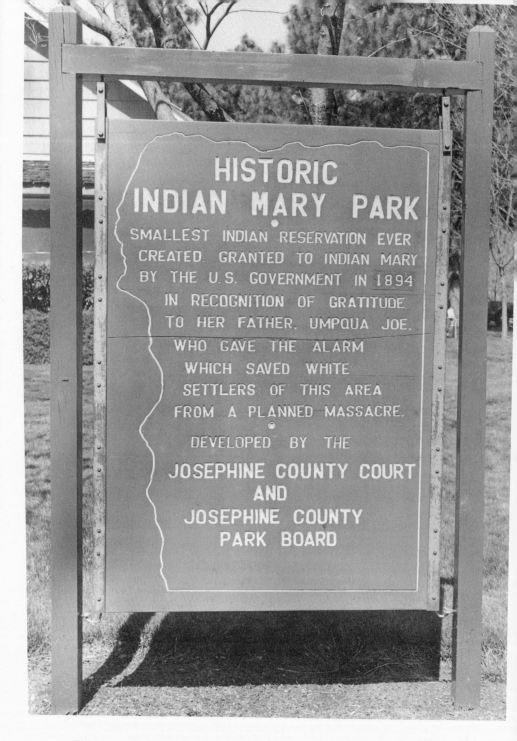

HISTORIC INDIAN MARY PARK

SMALLEST INDIAN RESERVATION EVER CREATED. GRANTED TO INDIAN MARY BY THE U.S. GOVERNMENT IN 1894 IN RECOGNITION OF GRATITUDE TO HER FATHER, UMPQUA JOE, WHO GAVE THE ALARM WHICH SAVED WHITE SETTLERS OF THIS AREA FROM A PLANNED MASSACRE.

DEVELOPED BY THE

JOSEPHINE COUNTY COURT AND JOSEPHINE COUNTY PARK BOARD

This handsome historical marker dedicated to Indian Mary and her father, Umpqua Joe, greets thousands of visitors annually at Indian Mary Park, in the Canyon Country of the famous Rogue River.

THE LEGEND OF INDIAN MARY
AND UMPQUA JOE

At two o'clock on a crisp autumn morning, October ninth, 1855, the quiet of the Rogue Valley was shattered by chilling victory cries of revenge. A wild, hostile party of Rogue Indians, raced out of the reservation at Table Rock, galloped across Chief Sam's Valley and began a deadly sweep along the Oregon-California Trail, killing and burning everything in their path.

Sixteen settlers and travelers along the pioneer road died that day — massacred — men, women and children. Property, crops and livestock, suffered thousands of dollars damage. The vicious raid was to mark the beginning of a new series of desperate struggles that would pit the white man against the Indian for more than three years: a continuing vengeful policy of extermination by both races, to determine who would live in the Valleys of the Rogue — the red man or the white man.

Excited by their success, the pillaging war party was quickly reinforced by three more groups of warriors. They were led by Chief George, of the lower Rogue country, Chief Limpy, of the Illinois Valley, and John, Chief of the Applegates. Their combined striking force was large enough that they could split their strength, and boldly attack settler's cabins along the trail as far north as the Twogood and Harkness' roadhouse, at the Grave Creek crossing, and down the Rogue to the high, rocky walls of the Canyon Country.

Couriers spurred frothy horses to Jacksonville with news of the bold assault. From there, more riders lashed fresh mounts to isolated settlements in the upper valley and the mines of Josephine Creek, Sterling Gulch and Galice Creek.

Josephine County Homestead

A hydraulic giant such as the one Dr. Louis Galice used in the creek named in his honor. The "Giant" was capable of sweeping hundreds of yards of gravel through a sluice box in one day. In 1851 Dr. Galice made rich discoveries with only a shovel and a gold pan.

Muddy, bewhiskered miners abandoned their claims, hurried out of the canyons and gulches and joined with the settlers. Together, they forted-up at the nearest staunchly-built cabin, with logs thick enough to check a musket ball, or turn the soft whisper of a feathered message of death.

The deceiving murmer of Rogue River spoke hardly above a whisper, as it slipped between the green lapels of fifty miles of gentle, sloping valleys. But once free of flat lands, it became a wild thing; bold, angry and defiant. Smashing head-on against a brooding barrier of dark, threatening mountains, and maddened by its confinement, it hurled its strength of angry froth and foam against everything that barred its way. Thrown back, shattered, white with fury, it quickly sidestepped, and attacked a new position.

Finally, in defeat, the mountainous wall of rock, yielded to the stubborn persistence of pounding water and permitted a narrow, rock-lined passage to open a way to the sea. Long ago, someone called the somber gorge, Hells Gate, and no one has argued with his choice.

Louis Galice, a French doctor, was one of the first to prospect in the wild country of the lower Rogue canyons. A few miles below Hells Gate, at the mouth of a creek slanting into the Rogue from a sharp fold in the mountains, he found coarse nuggets of bright yellow gold.

At that point the Rogue crowded through the rocky walls of a white-water chute, and then wrapped itself around a long, low river bar, covered with round boulders and discouraged brush, slanted by the slapping hand of spring freshets.

The queue of gold seekers trailing Galice, discovered that the creek and river, together, had nursed the bar for hundreds of years with generous pockets of heavy, flat pieces of gold.

Since those early days the rocky shelf has been called Skull Bar. The creek and mining community, born of the discovery, became known by the various names and spellings of, Gallice, Galeese, and Galliceburg. The name Skull Bar was the result of uncovering more than a hundred skulls and numerous human bones during mining operations. It was believed that the place had been an ancient burial ground, and that flood waters had scattered the bones across the bar.

Although the area had taken the name of its discoverer, it was not, in a true sense, a mining camp served by a trading post. The miners were completely dependent upon packers, who drove long strings of mules over the mountains from Paragon Bay, later to become Crescent City, or through the dangerous Umpqua and Cow Creek Canyons, from Scottsburg, the nearest saltwater shipping port at the head of tidewater on the Umpqua.

Even greenhorn farmers from the Willamette Valley, "with the proper amount of exertion", an expression writers of the era were fond of using, could wash from four, to a hundred dollars a day from gravel-lined crevices.

Such fabulous returns for their labors, sweetened the ears of new-comers in the saloons of Oregon City and across the bars of Jacksonville. But it failed to take into account the high prices of beans, bacon and gum boots, layed down at the diggin's.

During the winter of '52, when the flush of the rush was at its highest, and the high trails were blocked with snow banks and flooding streams, a packing charge of $1.00 a pound was considered normal. Such prices as $1.25 a pound for flour was not uncommon; $2.50 for a print of butter, $2.00 for salt, and tobacco soared to $4.50 for a pound tin, with precious little available at any price. Some packers even sold their mules at the end of their trips. An

This is Hells Gate, fifteen miles down river from Grants Pass. Through these portals of seething water, begin fifty miles of wilderness beauty, slashed from solid rock and washed with white water — truly one of the west's last outposts.

The first ferry at this site in the late 1850's was built and operated by Indian Joe Umpqua. Joe died in a violent shoot-out in 1886. His daughter, Mary, continued the operation until 1894. Pictured here is Hal Massie, canyon pioneer and members of his family. Building at rear, left, was Massie home. View is of the ferry landing on the north side of the river.

animal worth $20.00 in the Willamette Valley, might bring as much as $200.00 at Galice or Josephine Creek.

The miners along Galice Creek and Skull Bar had erected various kinds of shelters — crude cabins, shake shacks and tarpaulin lean-tos.

When a sweat-streaked horse and weary rider brought word from the upper valley of the latest Indian attacks, the miners hurriedly looked about for anything they could fortify and defend. Most of them had spent little of their precious time on permanent shelters, their driving force being to shovel as much pay dirt through their sluice boxes and Long Toms, as daylight hours would permit. Each day new hopefuls arrived and shouldered their way into the rich bonanza.

Two of the largest cabins on Skull Bar stood close together, not far from the river's edge. They had the distinction of being built of thick and sturdy logs, no doubt a mark of prestige to the discoverers of the two richest claims.

Knowing they were many hours of hard riding from the nearest help, about forty of the scattered miners gathered together to fortify and defend the two cabins. As always, they were poorly armed, there being "only about fifteen shots", in the whole outfit. Their arms consisted of thirteen old muzzleloaders and several pistols.

A few friendless Chinamen had been permitted to work some fringe ground at the lower end of the bar, well away from the whites. With some reluctance, the miners allowed the terrified Orientals to join with them in their fort.

A welcome addition to the nervous group were two friendly Indians, Joe Umpqua and his wife. Joe roamed with a small band of Indians living along the banks of upper Grave Creek. Even though his people were closely allied with the Umpqua tribe, they held themselves independent, had their own sub-leaders, and claimed no alliance with either the Umpquas or Rogues. Early historians referred to them, simply, as Grave Creeks.

Exactly why Joe decided to cast his lot with the white miners is not known. But in any case, Joe and his woman made their way down the river, one on each bank, as far as Skull Bar, warning the isolated miners that they had learned by Indian grapevine that a war party was planning an attack.

That was not the only time Joe befriended miners and settlers of the threatened areas.

T. McFadden Patton carried the mail between Deer Creek (Roseburg) and Jacksonville. Normal communications with all points north of the Six Bit House, at Wolf Creek, had been cut off since the massacre along the Oregon-California trail.

Except for heavily armed patrols, protecting daring express riders, carrying priority military and militia orders, nothing had moved through the perilous ambush miles of dreaded canyon.

Riders from the Willamette Valley were moving mail as far as the Six Bit House, without problems. There, it was piling up.

Patton appealed to Captain Andrew Jackson Smith, commander of Fort Lane, near Table Rock, for an armed escort to accompany him as far as the Six Bit House, with pouches of mail going north. From that point, northward, there seemed to be little danger of attack, and the escort could return to Fort Lane guarding the Jacksonville mail. He was provided with five heavily armed dragoons.

McFadden wrote a vivid account of his canyon adventures. Part of his chronicle gave these interesting notes about Joe Umpqua:

"Umpqua Joe told Dr. Paxton at the Six Bit House that all of the Indians of Shasta, Klamath, Horse Creek, (Klamath River area) Grave Creek and Rogue River had combined . . . to murder all the whites . . . Umpqua Joe, who is a friendly Indian, was Fremont's guide and has always fought on the side of the whites."

It is interesting to note the reversal of Joe's name. Depending upon the historian, he was called Umpqua Joe, or Joe Umpqua.

The apprehensive miners on Skull Bar worked feverishly to fortify their position, cutting away the surrounding willows and brush, and throwing-up a breastwork of logs and driftwood. Then, in front of their make-shift fort, they dug a trench, deep enough to shelter a man laying flat on his belly. It was intended as a sort of advance post to reinforce the log parapet.

While these preparations were in progress, the miners were overjoyed at the arrival of a volunteer force from the upper valley of some thirty-seven men, commanded by Captain W. B. Lewis.

Two more miners managed to slip into the fort and reported they had discovered "Indian sign", indicating the Rogues had gathered together a large force and were preparing to attack.

Sergeant Israel Adams, of the volunteers, ventured to creep out and scout the position of the enemy. He had wormed his way no more than a hundred feet, when he found himself pinned down by a smother of whining bullets.

As the besieged miners had feared, their position on the unprotected bar was not going to be easy to defend. Although the river afforded some protection at their rear, the Indians could approach the little stronghold through cover of alders, willows and hazel brush, as well as, fire into their fort from the heights of the sloping canyon walls.

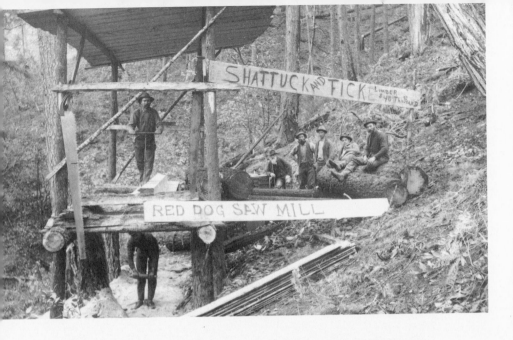

It is hard to imagine a more laborsome method of manufacturing lumber than the old whip-saw-mill. This mill was built on a hillside so logs could be rolled right on the sawing platform.

There were a few years, during the time between wagon and automobile/truck transportation in which the traction steam engine filled the need for hauling heavy loads. The time was about 1905 to 1910, this is a monster of an age gone by.

As rifle balls poured across the pinned-down sergeant, J. W. Pickett and six others volunteered to go to his rescue. Scampering across the open space they were met by a withering fire from an unseen enemy, sprouting from a score of smoke puffs along the hillside. Pickett was struck by a ball that tore its way completely through the left side of his body. His companions were able to drag him to a place of safety, but he died later that same day. Pickett Creek was named for this honored pioneer.

With no defense against the vicious crossfire whistling over them, they began an inch by inch retreat back to their fort. More Indian slugs found their mark.

Seeing the dangerous predicament of their comrades, Lieutenant W. A. J. Moore and five volunteers made a wild dash to the freshly-dug trench to cover the retreating men. Dragging their wounded companions across the rocky ground, Pickett's party was finally able to tumble into the trench with their protectors.

For four hours the duel continued. The pinned-down men in the trench could do little more than aim at blobs of blue smoke rolling from behind trees, brush and rocks. The shower of lead cascading into their shallow dugout made their post more and more dangerous. Two more defenders were hit, one critically, the other in the knee. Lieutenant Moore received two wounds. The order was given to retreat to the cabins.

Slowly, they craw-fished toward their pitiful fort, the unwounded tugging and dragging their suffering comrades behind them. Before they could reach safety, another of the rescuers was knocked out of action when a slug tore a bloody groove across his jaw. Finally, shattered and bleeding and with nearly every man wounded, they were pulled into the protection of the fort.

The Indians were quick to close in and take advantage of the retreat. One by one, they set fire to the remaining miner's huts. Only the crowded cabins under attack remained. The distressed defenders were hard pressed to keep flaming arrows landing on the roof, from burning their fort down around their ears. Several times they were forced to crawl outside, exposing themselves to enemy fire, while they beat out spreading flames.

And then the bar exploded with yelping Indians! The stentorian roll of Chief John's voice, echoed again and again, as rocky walls hurled back his shouted orders. The slanted face of the canyon squirmed with warriors like a hill of red ants kicked in anger. Screaming, firing, dodging — a ragged wave of hate and death, hideously painted, each wearing a single white feather in his headband, charged against the miner's holdout. A score of leaping braves scurried to the abandoned trench and turned that defense site into a point of attack. Chief John's voice rolled again, shouting words of encouragement to his attacking force. Close behind him came Chiefs George and Limpy, leading more than eighty fanatic warriors.

The defenders were ready. A screen of lead met the oncoming horde full in the face. Bloodcurdling screams were driven back into red throats. Rogues staggered, faltered, fell — and the line broke. As quickly as they had mounted their charge they scampered for safety. For a moment there was only ringing silence, and then a hoarse victory cheer was raised from throats parched by a sharp sear of powder smoke.

During the charge, somebody, whether by luck or superior marksmanship, we shall never know, dropped a huge warrior leading the pack. It was later learned that he was not a Rogue, but a much respected Shasta, who had joined with his cousins to support their war against the common invader.

His death served to instill a fresh note of caution among the attackers. Instead of following with another charge, they seemed satisfied to continue the attack with rifle fire, interspersed with attempts to burn the stubborn stronghold with flaming arrows.

But the defenders had also suffered heavy losses. A slug had smashed its way through the clay chinking of the log walls and struck Private Sam Sanders squarely in the head, killing him instantly. Umpqua Joe had also been wounded, but the injury was not serious.

The hours wore on. Firing was continuous. Hundreds of Indian slugs slammed against the splintered logs. Although no one voiced an opinion, there were few among them who believed they would be able to hold out against another charge as vicious as the one they had just weathered.

Throughout the remaining hours of daylight, bouncing echoes of gunfire boomed against the canyon walls. Occasionally, the firing would stop and instead of lead, curses and threats were hurled across the narrow open space. Threatening boasts, interpreted by Umpqua Joe's woman, goaded the whites with the promise, they would soon be ready to take their scalps and burn their cabins.

Not to be outdone, the defenders returned the challenge, easily outclassing the Rogues with choice insults, sprinkled liberally with generous allusions concerning their ancestral heritage. But the exchange of taunts and abuse failed to excite either side into making foolhardy moves.

When the fading rays of last light deserted the frowning gorge, the Indians, to the surprise of the miners, broke the siege by withdrawing. In the paleness of cold starlight they could see vague forms moving about in the distance, apparently carrying dead or wounded.

The relieved miners worked all night improving their defenses. They tore up the puncheon floor, gouged out dirt and threw it against the log walls for added protection. Sacks of flour received only a few days before were piled on the dirt abutment. Outside, it was quiet, only lonesome river sounds and a cry of nighthawks broke the silence.

When false dawn first touched the canyon the Rogues returned, and with what seemed a determination to have the last word, fired a few ineffectual shots into the beleaguered cabins and disappeared again.

Slowly, morning light settled to the ground. The bodies of six Indians could be seen scattered across the rocky battlefield near the trench. Cautiously, muskets ready, they ventured from the dimness of their stronghold, eyes blinking against the brash new light.

The canyon's high walls pressed a strange feeling of quietness in upon them. A gentle quiver of water sounds, mixed with ringing in their ears. And the familiar smell of the river was there again, instead of powder stench.

Although they had withstood the siege, they had won no victory. Two volunteers were dead, two were mortally wounded and seven were seriously wounded.

There was little solace in the facts learned from the fight. Certainly, the position at Skull Bar, or for that matter, any position in the canyon could not be defended. The surprisingly strong show of arms and ammunition indicated that the Rogues had prepared for just such action for a long time. And, most discouraging of all, the Indians had melted away into the mountains, free to emerge and strike again where least expected.

In his report of the battle to Colonel Ross, Captain Lewis told the story just as he and his men had lived it. He made no attempt to minimize the strength and viciousness of the attack, or the seriousness of their position. His accounting paid tribute to a group of valiant men, and respect for a shrewd and determined enemy.

"It was", he declared, "the hardest fought battle ever to take place this side of the Rocky Mountains, with over 1500 shots being fired by the enemy in one day."

In the years that followed the Indian wars, not everyone in the Rogue Country was poisoned with a lasting hatred for those with dark skin. To show their appreciation for his co-operation, the settlers and miners asked that Umpqua Joe and his woman be allowed to remain in their native southern Oregon, instead of being banned to a reservation with the rest of the Rogues and Umpquas.

The saga of Umpqua Joe does not fade into oblivion after the battle of Skull Bar, as did the surviving remnants of the once proud tribe that called the Rogue their own.

Joe had always proven to be a peaceful man. Surrounded by the last raw edge of Oregon's frontier and the savagery that was a part of it, a series of wild and explosive events were thrust upon him. Oddly enough, they led to the white man establishing a monument of peace and beauty, befitting the vanished people he represented. Violent, bloody, and ending in death, his is a true story of the old west, matching the time, the country and the people.

When the conflict and bloodshed of the Indian wars were finally over, Joe "squatted on" a piece of high river bank, not far upstream from the mouth of Galice Creek and Skull Bar. He built a little one room log cabin, in the center of an open flat, hunted, fished, raised a garden and planted a few fruit trees in the rich river loam.

At regular intervals Joe's wife presented him with a baby — two girls and a boy. The first girl was called Mary, a name as popular with the Indians as it was with the pioneers. The second girl was named Betsy, and the boy became known as Kelsay Joe. Young Joe was named after an early Oregon pioneer.

John Kelsay was born in Kentucky and educated in Missouri. At age 26, he was admitted to the bar and served a term in the Missouri Legislature. He crossed the plains in 1853 and settled in Corvallis.

In response to urgent pleas from harassed settlers and miners of southern Oregon, Governor Curry authorized that volunteer companies be raised, under authority of the Territorial Militia, to serve in the Rogue Valley. Kelsay was commissioned a Captain. In the spring of 1856, he recruited a company of volunteers from Benton County.

They marched from Corvallis to Fort Leland, at the Grave Creek crossing, and then with other companies, into the Rogue Canyon Country, hoping to trap Chief John and his warriors in the Mule Creek-Big Meadows area. The wily old chief eluded Kelsay and fled with his warriors, women and children, deeper into the unknown chasms of the lower Rogue.

Later, Kelsay became a Colonel, helped write, and was a signer of Oregon's Constitution, a Justice of the Supreme Court of Oregon, and was named ambassador to India.

Kelsey Creek, Kelsey Peak, and Kelsey Canyon, all in the Mule Creek area, were named in honor of this much respected pioneer. The difference in spelling of his last name, is only one of the many such instances that appear in southern Oregon history.

Historians have failed to record, exactly why Umpqua Joe named his only son after Kelsay, but it was common practice in those days, for Indians to take the name of an admired "white warrior".

Miners continued to stream into the canyon country, prospecting every creek that emptied into the Rogue. For a time, Joe rowed them back and forth across the river, but he soon realized that he needed a ferry to transport supplies and animals.

The river banks being gentle enough for landings below his cabin and across the river where the trail ended, he built a crude, flat-bottomed, current operated raft-like ferry. His crossing soon became a part of the canyon scene.

Joe had seen much violence and bloodshed in his life as a scout, and later during the Indian wars, in his attempts to befriend the white man. After settling on a piece of quiet river land and becoming a responsible ferry operator it would seem that the remainder of his days should have been spent in peace.

A long forgotten incident, buried for more than a hundred years in dusty court records, opened a page that shrouded Joe's life in still more violence and mystery. The occurrence took place in 1869, sixteen years before Grants Pass became a town or had a newspaper. Some of the details have been lost, there being only sketchy and incomplete court records to tell the story.

At Kerbyville, then the County seat for Josephine County, a grand jury returned the following indictment for the crime of manslaughter.

"The said Umpqua Joe on the 13th. day of July, 1869 in the County aforesaid voluntarily killed A. Morton by shooting him with a gun whereby he was then and there mortally wounded, of which mortal wound then and there received, he the said A. Morton on the said 13th. day of July 1869 died."

Joe was arrested by Sheriff Daniel Green and taken to Kerbyville to await action in the next term of circuit court, scheduled for October 1870. It is apparent from court records that Joe had many good and faithful friends who immediately made the long horseback trip from Galiceburg to Kerbyville and jointly bonded themselves for the sum of $1,000.00 bail for Joe's release. Several witnesses also volunteered to testify in his behalf.

Among the seven bondsmen were such well known citizens as James N. Vannoy, fellow ferry operator on

Rogue River at old Fort Vannoy; J. G. Adams, merchant at Galiceburg and Wm. Lind hotel keeper.

The following entry from a timeworn Josephine County Circuit Court Journal, describes the resulting action in the legal mood of an age gone by, penned with the beauty and free flowing flourish of yesteryears' handwriting.

"Be it remembered that at a Circuit Court of the State of Oregon for the County of Josephine, began and held at Kerbyville on Monday the 24th. day of October A.D. 1870, at which were present Hon. P.P. Prim, judge, Chas. Hughes, clerk, Dan'l Green, sheriff and H. K. Hanna Dist. Atty. at which time the following proceedings were had."

State of Oregon   Indictment for
vs   Manslauter
Umpqua Joe

"Now at this day comes the State by H. K. Hanna Esqr. Dist. Atty. and the defendent comes also in proper person and by E. B. and J. F. Watson and Wm. Willis Esqrs. his attorneys.

And a jury comes also ، . . Twelve in all, good and lawful men of the County, duly impannelled and sworn to well and truly try the issue between the State and the defendent, and after hearing the testimony of the witnesses, the arguments of Counsel, as well for the defendent as the State, and also the Charge of the Court, retired under the charge of a sworn officer to consider of their verdict.

After a short absence they returned into Court and returned the following verdict — 'we the jury find the prisoner not guilty as charged' . . .

It is therefore ordered that said defendent be discharged from custody and that his bail be exonerated."

As time passed, Joe's children grew into young adulthood. Betsy married an Indian lad from the Trinity River country of northern California. To keep the family namesake unbroken, it was handy to call him Trinity Joe.

Umpqua Joe's woman died, but the time and manner of her death has been lost.

An outsider, said to be from British crown territory, now British Columbia, named Albert Peco, an uncertain mixture of Indian, French and Spanish, took Mary for his wife. They were married by Justice of the Peace, P. S. W. Smith at his home in Grants Pass, May 17, 1885. Mary's name is recorded on the marriage certificate as "Mary Umpqua."

The next trial of sorrow to fall on the aging shoulders of Umpqua Joe was the death of his son, Kelsay Joe, Aug. 28, 1884. Young Joe's death was the result of an argument that erupted, according to witnesses, in a Front Street saloon. Time has erased the actual cause of the affair, but in every other respect it satisfies the needs of a fictional thriller — a typical wild west brawl in a rough-shod frontier town.

The fight began when Joe pulled a knife on George R. Justus, owner of the Grants Pass Livery and Feed Stable. Justus was unarmed and immediately withdrew, with Joe in hot pursuit. They raced down the dusty street, Joe brandishing his knife and Justus fleeing for his life. The threatened man reached the sanctuary of his home, rushed inside, locked the door and armed himself with a pistol.

Joe gave up the chase and "passed on down the street." But the enraged Justus was not content to let the affair end without redeeming his honor. "He returned to the street, where he again met the Indian and hostilities were renewed."

Joe, seeing the wild eyed Justus, with pistol pointed threateningly in his direction knew his knife was no match for the infuriated man. He whirled and ran. Justus commenced firing. "Hurling a stream of bullets at his adversary, several of which took effect."

Somebody hurried the news to the sheriff, who immediately placed Justus under arrest. Young Joe was carried to a nearby house, where "citizens gave him the best of attention and Dr. W. H. Flanagan was called." From the nature of his wounds the doctor had grave doubts that Joe would survive.

Three days after the shooting, Justice of the Peace Volney Colvig, charged that Justus be confined and held without bail for grand jury action. At that time, Josephine County Circuit Court cases were being tried in Jacksonville.

Constable Morris took the prisoner to Jacksonville, where he was lodged in jail, which, complained the editor of the Jacksonville Democratic Times, "already has four inmates with no room for any more." Justus was held against a possible charge of murder.

Exactly a month later, August 28th., Kelsay Joe died. The Jacksonville paper carried this brief account: "He was the son of Indian Joe, who runs a ferryboat on Rogue River and was about 21 years of age at the time of his death."

During the next regular term of Circuit Court, November 11, 1884, T. B. Kent District Attorney, made the following charge:

"George R. Justus is accused by the Grand Jury of the County of Jackson and the State of Oregon, by this indictment, of the crime of murder in the first degree. Committed as follows.

The said George R. Justus on the 28th day of July A.D. 1884 . . . purposely and of deliberate and premeditated malice killed William Joseph Umpqua, then and there shooting him with a pistol, contrary to the statute in such cases made and provided for and against the peace and dignity of the State of Oregon."

However, the defendant's attorney, H. K. Hanna, appealed the murder charge and was successful in getting it reduced to manslaughter.

Witnesses called and testifying in the case were Dr. W. H. Flanagan, Grants Pass pioneer physician, Joseph Umpqua, A. H. Grigsby, D. G. Davis, John Every, Dr. G. H. Aiken and J. G. Moon.

George R. Justus was convicted and sentenced to ten years imprisonment in the penitentiary of the State of Oregon, at Salem, "and that the defendant pay a fine of five dollars, and the plaintiff, the State of Oregon, do have and recover of and from the defendant his costs and disbursements of this suit to be taxed."

Attorney Hanna then petitioned for a new trial for Justus, but it was denied by Judge Webster.

Before going to the penitentiary Justus sold his livery stable to Henry Thornton, who operated it for several years under the name of, Grants Pass Livery Stable, H. Thornton and son proprietors.

After the death of his son, Joe's life slipped into a hazy stream of memory pictures. He was filled with a hollow ache of loneliness, as he remembered the long-ago days when he was a strong young man, respected as a scout and appreciated by the whites.

Pushed aside by the insolence of new and greedy gold seekers and the swift passage of time, the old man sought occasional solace in Grants Pass. There he would quietly seek-out Lee Jack, an understanding Chinaman, who, for a price, always had a bottle of whiskey for his Indian friends.

Joe would then make the rounds of the shabby saloons framing the railroad tracks, willing to spend as much time in each establishment, as he could get listeners.

As his spirits soared and the bottle dropped, he would let out an occasional war whoop and showing the same generosity to all, launch into his favorite subject.

He told his bored listeners how he fought the Rogues across the very ground on which they stood, and that he was twice wounded and his pardner killed. Forgetting that he was living thirty years in the past, he reminded them that they would all be dead, if it hadn't been for his help. It proved, he said, that he was a very smart man for joining with the whites, for he was much alive and the Rogues all dead. And as final proof that he was still the man he claimed to be, he let it be known that he was in the market for a young, white wife. Tolerated as long as patience lasted, some old timer would take him by the arm, escort him to the door, deposit him on the boardwalk and point him down the street.

In October, 1886, thirty years after the days of his memories, Joe made one of his periodic trips to Grants Pass. It was to be his last. About a month later, November 13th, he and his son-in-law, Albert Peco, engaged in a shoot-out that was to equal any ever dreamed by writers of western fiction.

It all started over a dog. A miner in the Galice area owned a beautiful and intelligent St. Bernard, named Faust. The huge animal was a devoted companion and a valuable asset to his owner. His master would write a note, put it in a basket and send the faithful animal to the trading post. If other dogs had the nerve to challenge Faust, he would carefully put his basket on the ground, bowl them over a few times with his huge shoulders and then with a satisfied look of dog superiority, continue with his errand.

Happy as only a well loved dog could be, Faust's world crumbled around him when his master moved from the sweaty, little mining community to Grants Pass. The scroungy dogs and muddy alleys of city life offered little of interest to a camp dog, accustomed to the daily challenge of callous gold mines.

After a few days of backyard prowling and half-hearted cat chasing, he struck out for his old home. His owner brought him back to town several times, but Faust had a mind of his own. Finally, his master gave up, and Faust found kindness, plenty to eat, and a new home with Umpqua Joe. Joe loved the big dog and placed him second in importance of all his possessions, only to his rifle.

For a long time Albert Peco had been saving a few pennies from each of his packing jobs to buy a new rifle. The long awaited day finally arrived. He went to Grants Pass and picked out a shiny, new Marlin. He bought a few supplies, some ammunition, paid Lee Jack a visit and headed for home. He could hardly wait to get out of town, so he could try his new gun. He was pleased with its accuracy, and its balance and "feel".

When he got back to the ranch the first thing Peco did was to show Joe his new possession. He broke out the bottle and they had a few drinks. Then they went off toward the river for some target practice. They both shot the gun, but it was Peco who was the marksman. After breaking every empty whiskey bottle Joe tossed into the swirling eddy below the riffle, they both agreed that he had made a good choice and returned to the cabin.

They played several games of cards while they worked on the bottle. Whiskey brought out a mean streak in Peco; a streak that was shallow enough even when he was sober. Several times he had whipped himself into a savage frenzy of uncontrollable anger, threatening to shoot anybody that dared his nasty disposition and forcing the whole family to flee for their lives. Both Joe and Mary feared and hated him.

While the card game was in progress, the excited barking of dogs drew Peco to the window. Faust and a visting friend were having some fun chasing one of Peco's pack mules. Furious, the soggy Peco spit out a string of unintelligible French and Spanish oaths. Grabbing his new rifle he ran outside and began firing. With only three shots he killed both of the running dogs. Joe saw his great St. Bernard plow his face into the ground and roll over and over, rag limp.

Joe seized his old Yager, ran to the door and fired a load of birdshot into the air. Whirling back into the cabin he slammed the door, secured it with a heavy chain and loaded the ancient weapon with buckshot.

At the sound of Joe's shot, Peco lurched toward the cabin. Finding the door chained against him, he tried to force it open. From the other side, Joe warned him not to come in — to go away and leave him alone. Insane with whiskey madness, Peco smashed the door down and plunged into the little room. Joe fired as the lunging form framed the splintered doorway.

The inquest report of the shoot-out described it this way:

"The entire charge of buckshot entered Peco's body at the left groin, severing the phemoral artery and leaving a hole through him nearly as large as a man's fist. Peco fell, with his hip shattered to pieces, and his life's blood rushing from his body. But he fired three shots with startling rapidity and unerring aim, one of which tore Joe's heart to shreds, the second passed through his body, entering the left side of the back and coming out below the left nipple. The third shot was not accounted for. Both men fell dead at the same instant."

Mary and Betsy were huddled in a corner of the room when the shooting began. Terror stricken, they both ran outside, sure that Peco would turn his gun on them. When no more shots came from the cabin, they ventured back to

Mining crew clears away for the construction of a water flume down a steep hillside.

Rogue Valley Stages used this stop to change horses & rest passengers at Kerbyville, on the Grants Pass — Crescent City run.

More than a century ago, courageous pioneers ventured into this rocky maze of forbidden canyons to search for gold. Where once roamed only wild animals and free Indians, modern pioneers now find something more precious than gold — an unspoiled world of natural beauty, sweetened with a taste of peace and solitude.

No ferry crossing in early-day Oregon Country served a more colorful period of pioneer history than did this one across the Rogue River near the old mining district of Galice Creek. A vicious Indian attack, a wild scramble for new-found gold and a series of unbelievable acts of violence, made this moody frontier of brooding canyons the last in the west to feel the slow touch of civilization. Photo shows Merlin-Galice stage mid-river, on a regular run to the mines. Log and shake structure at upper right was "ferry cabin".

witness, "a scene that was one of blood and desperation carried to the utmost extreme."

Again they fled outside, wailing and screaming. When some degree of calmness returned, Mary knew she must notify the sheriff. She caught a horse and mounting bare-back, started on a lope for the Anderson Vannoy ranch.

It was a wild and eerie ride. The first few miles were over a twisting, narrow trail, across rough and rocky hills hanging above the river bluffs. Then she galloped another eleven miles to the old Vannoy ferry site, along a make-believe, wagon-track road, through stands of timber and manzanita brush. The few lonely ranchers along the Rogue, did not soon forget that scary night, with its ghostly manifestation of a pounding white horse and a wailing Indian girl, disturbing the sleepy solitude of the lower valley.

From the ferry, Holman Peter, a neighboring farmer, and duly appointed constable carried the news of the double killing from Vannoys to town, arriving about nine o'clock. Mary returned home.

Sheriff Tom Patterson, being sick and unable to make the long trip, asked Justice of the Peace, John Goodell, to gather a party of citizens, go to the scene of the tragedy and hold an inquest.

In less than an hour, Goodell had summoned his brother-in-law, Dr. F. W. Van Dyke and professor H. L. Benson, of the Grants Pass Academy.

From Smith Brothers Stable, he hired a team and wagon, and Bob Smith to do the driving. Holman Peter, Ira Sparlin, and Anderson Vannoy completed the inquest party.

At Hog Creek, where the road ended, they pounded on the door of "Uncle" Billy Crow's cabin. Billy quickly dressed and agreed to accompany the party. Billy's home

No one worked harder and reaped less than the sturdy pioneers of Josephine County.

Gold was not the only valuable mineral to be found in the rich Galice mining area. In 1910 extensive deposits of copper ore, also containing paying amounts of gold and silver, were discovered at Almeda, a few miles below Galice Creek. Pictured here is a newly completed bridge, spanning the white, rushing waters of the Rogue, with construction of mine's smelter buildings well under way.

was a wayside stop on the Galice trail and offered a meal and a bed to canyon travelers.

Carrying coal oil lanterns, they walked in a circle of funeral shadows the rest of the way to the ferry landing, arriving at three o'clock in the morning. Mary heard their shouts and brought the ferry across the river.

Dr. Van Dyke examined the bodies, while Goodell asked questions of the only witnesses. After a brief look, the rest of the sickened men waited outside, smoking, and talking in whispered tones.

Finally, with the doctor and Goodell finished, the weary party retraced their steps to Hog Creek and then drowsed their way back to Grants Pass in the slow skylight of a gray November morning.

It is recorded that the coroner's jurors were paid $4.40 for their night's work, except Holman Peter and Anderson Vannoy, who received only $3.80, their travel time having been less than the others. Mary and Betsy each received $1.50 witness fees.

And where are Umpqua Joe and Albert Peco buried? No one knows for sure. Some think that Rogue River tried to solve the mystery, in its own way, but others contend it only succeeded in clouding the question more.

In 1912, Hal Massie, pioneer stage driver on the Merlin-Galice run made an interesting find. After a period of high water had overrun the Rogue's banks, he noticed a grave-like depression where there had been none before, on the north side of the river, not far from an old shack known as the "ferry house".

He and his sister Mable, scooped out some sand and gravel and uncovered the remains of a rough, whip-sawn, board coffin containing human bones.

There seemed to be little doubt that the unmarked grave was that of an unknown Indian. None of the old timers could recall any white man having been buried on that side of the river. Could the grave have been the last resting place of Umpqua Joe, or perhaps, Albert Peco?

Another story of finding ancient graves in the same area some thirty years later, is told by A. E. "Doc" Yarbrough, a native son of Josephine county. When he was a lad of fifteen "Doc" drove team and wagon for George Elder, pioneer storekeeper at Waldo, first county seat of Josephine county, and center of some of southern Oregon's richest gold discoveries.

"Doc" and another old timer, Art Colvin, were salmon fishing on the north side of the river, about 200 yards below the previous steel, Hells Gate bridge, (not the present structure) when "Doc" discovered two open graves.

Another high water run-off, this time from heavy rains cascading down the steep face of the canyon slope had washed away a considerable amount of dirt and gravel, exposing two coffins. Each contained undisturbed skeletons. The crudely built coffins had been fashioned from thick, rough planks split from cedar logs.

It was generally agreed that the graves were those of Indians, the condition of the planks indicating that they could have been in the ground since the turn of the century, possibly longer.

Again there was conjecture that the graves could have been those of Albert Peco and Umpqua Joe.

There is a third speculation about the lost graves, that seems to be the most logical. Piecing together several stories by old timers and early historians, there is more than a casual amount of information indicating that Umpqua Joe and Albert Peco were buried on Joe's old ranch, quite possibly, not far from the present boat landing at Indian Mary Park. Although the graves have been lost, at least two old timers have left stories, that the burials took place on the property.

It seems that the answer to their last resting place is likely to be buried with other lost pages in the early-day history of the wild Canyon Country.

After the double tragedy, Mary and her sister decided to remain at the ranch and continue operating the ferry. An abundant garden provided a great deal of their food. The sweeping riffle below the cabin swirled into a deep, green eddy, where rested the salmon and steelhead before continuing their up-river journey to spawning beds. The peach trees that Joe had set-out, flourished in the sandy river loam. The sheltering canyon walls held back the killing frost of late spring, and the crop was usually heavy and the fruit large and delicious. It found a ready market.

On November 30, 1886, eighteen days after her father's death, Mary filed a first homestead application in the U. S. Land Office at Roseburg, Oregon, on the river property he had "squatted on" thirty years before. The application certified that the survey contained 72 and 34/100 acres.

An affidavit was also filed with the county clerk of Josephine county. It reads as follows:

"I, Mary Peco, of Galice Creek, Josephine Co. Ore., having filed my homestead application . . . do solemnly swear that I am an Indian formerly of the Rogue River tribe, that I was born in the United States, that I have abandoned my relations with that tribe and adopted the habits and pursuits of civilized life, that I am a widow and at the head of a family. I am now residing on the land I desire to enter, and that I have made a bona fide improvement and settled thereon; that settlement was commenced in 1855, that my improvements consist of a log house, log barn, five acres in orchard and thirty acres in cultivation and under fence, and that the value is $500.00.

her

(Signed) Mary X Peco

mark

Records indicate that Mary married a second time. On September 16, 1889, Justice of the Peace, Abe Axtell, in his office in Grants Pass, "joined in lawful wedlock, Jackson Peters and Mary Peco, with their mutual consent."

Her new husband was an Indian, said to be a native of the Jacksonville area, and was known locally as "Jacksonville Petus." Mary is credited with changing, Petus, to Peters, a name more in keeping with her wishes to foresake, completely, her Indian heritage, for the white man's style of living.

The canyon people, not being so particular, saw no need for a name change and kept the tradition simple, by calling him Joe Peters.

Things went well enough for two or three years. Joe often went on packing, hunting and prospecting trips with a white, part-time miner, whose name is remembered by old timers as Jack Fairfield. He was said to have been fair-complexioned and of German ancestory.

Fairfield looked with envy on the little ranch, nestled in its beautiful setting. He liked what he saw; a comfortable cabin, a fine orchard, and a good garden — chickens, hogs, and all of the trimmings. Fishing was excellent. Deer and bear could be killed in the orchard, without leaving the shelter of the cabin porch. In all the canyon, it was one of the few places where the stern rock walls permitted a piece of level ground and good soil — safe from the reach of high waters.

Fairfield's acquisition was a simple one. He ran Joe off and moved in. Mary was delighted. She told friends: "Me no love Joe, me love white man."

Canyon life was smooth and without incident for about a year, then Fairfield disappeared. Betsy also dropped from sight. It is remembered that she and Trinity Joe returned to the Trinity River country of northern California.

For a time, Mary continued to run the ferry, and became a part of the canyon scene, as her father had before her. She asked little of anyone and accepted life as it came.

Season after season, Spring Beauties graced the hard face of the ageless canyon country, but only its people felt the swift passage of time.

Mary stepped aside, and in her place there would be many ferry operators pole the awkward craft from the grasp of sandy banks, into the pull of downward current.

Her children were reaching school age, Richard was about ten, Rosetta seven, David three or four, and Lillian a baby of about one year.

It became harder and harder for Mary to scratch out a living for her family. She was determined that her children should attend school and get an education that she had been denied. She decided that her only course was to move to town, where she would have a much better chance of finding work.

She leased her ranch to William Massie, another canyon pioneer, who owned land adjoining hers, down-river. Massie enlarged the orchard, planting more peach trees.

In 1894, when Mary was forty-two, she moved from the only home she had ever known, to a county owned, unpainted house, in the southwestern outskirts of Grants Pass.

That same year she received a government title to her father's canyon property. It was granted under provisions of an, "Act of Congress, July 4, 1884", entitled, "An Act making appropriations for the current and contingent expenses of the Indian Department, and for fulfilling treaty stipulations with various Indian Tribes for the year ending June thirtieth, eighteen hundred and eighty-five, and for other purposes, the claim of Mary Peters, formerly Mary Peco, and Indian, has been established and duly consummated in conformity to law . . . Hereby declares that it

During pioneer days in the Rogue Valley, Grants Pass was miner's headquarters. In 1905 — the little rough and unshod town had 12 saloons. The Miners Exchange at the corner of "G" and 5th Street was one of the better establishments.

Artesian wells were not uncommon in early Grants Pass. One such well, on west "G" street near Gilbert Creek, bubbled with pure, sweet water and was responsible for the first brewery in the valley in 1886. Customers lineup in the old Brewery Saloon to pass judgment on the local product.

does and will hold the land, described, for the period of twenty-five years, in trust, for the sole use and benefit of the said Mary Peters, or in case of her decease, of her heirs . . . "

The document was signed by President Grover Cleveland.

The following news item appeared in the Grants Pass Oregon Observer, December 15, 1894:

"Mary Peco, the Indian woman familiarly known as "Mary" who claims a little farm down Rogue River, has at last got title to her land, but it is not perfect. Her deed signed by President Cleveland is a trust deed and provides that patent absolute shall not issue over twenty-five years. Mary and her heirs can hold and cultivate the land until then. It is in effect the establishment of a small Indian reservation in Josephine county under government protection."

It was no easy task for an Indian woman to find work in the white man's town. But Mary was persistent and a hard worker and it wasn't long until she was "taking in" washings from several families.

Pauline Shier is the granddaughter of pioneer James and Margaret Savage, who in 1853 settled on a donation claim along the banks of Rogue River, just above present-day Savage Rapids dam. The dam and Savage Creek are named in their honor. Pauline remembers when she was a small child, her mother telling stories about Mary doing their family washing.

Mary's washing was always outstanding. Somehow, she achieved a wash that had a brightness of its own — pioneer style.

It was true. Mary did have a secret of her own; a long forgotten washing aid that may have been the forerunner of some of our much exploited, modern-day laundry products.

Early day Front Street in Grants Pass not only provided a generous choice of meat markets and saloons, but modern hotels and restaurants were available to make a gold miner's visit to town a memorable event.

Some photographer from days gone by, stops to record this picture of a comfortable and well built cabin.

She made a solution by boiling peach leaves and sal soda. When added to the wash water and final rinse, the clothes had the distinction of being the cleanest, whitest, and best smelling in all the valley. Mary's mixture was the equivalent of "Javelle Water", a product originally introduced in France, in those early days, and often used in washings as a combination disinfectant and deodorizer. Other necessary ingredients, not mentioned, were an abundance of strong, homemade soap, and hours of backbreaking knuckle-bruising washboard exercise.

Time moves faster than memories. Tragedy struck again at Mary's family, this time her two sons. In those days of hardships, diphtheria was still a dreaded and deadly killer of children. During the winter of 1904, its choking fingers reached into many homes across the Rogue Valley. On May 24th., Richard, Mary's oldest died. At the bottom of his death notice was appended, without explanation, these sad and poignant words: "Indian Mary has been sadly afflicted, having also lost her younger son (David) on April 9."

Mary settled into the quiet routine of the sleepy little town. She and her daughters joined the Salvation Army and became familiar and faithful members in its cause.

There are a few old timers who still remember when the little group marched to the beat of a big bass drum from the "army hall" on west Front Street, to the corner of Sixth, where they would engage in the "Sunday evening terrible battle for souls."

A few street-loungers always gathered on the sidewalk, leaned against the bank building and listened to the hymns and confessions. But the real convincers were the shrill-pitched notes of the cornet and the boom of the big drum, banging away at listener's ears and sinner's conscience.

After the tambourine had been passed and services were over, the measured beat of the drum would melt away in the dim glow of Front Street's cluster lights.

As Mary marched in drum-beat step, back to the board benches of their little worship hall, her eyes were straight ahead as she passed the shoddy saloons where her brother, Kelsay, died in violence, and her father had spun his tales of happier days.

Rosetta and Lillian, or Lilly, as she was called, so enjoyed church activities, especially Christmas and holiday musicals, that they also attended the Methodist Sunday school.

Lilly was a pretty little girl, bright and eager. When she was just four years old she was chosen to take part in a special children's program. Much time was spent coaching her to sing a solo for Sunday School Children's Day. She practiced the verse, over and over, and was finally declared ready for her performance.

Amos Voorhies, editor of the Grants Pass Courier, recalled the amusing incident in a story about the program, in an April, 1910, issue.

"Lilly sang a solo but not knowing when to stop, she sang it over three times. It caused considerable merriment, but everyone was well pleased with her part of the entertainment."

Rosetta and Lilly attended Grants Pass grade schools. When Rosetta reached high school age, she enrolled in the Chemawa Indian School, at Salem, completing four years of study. Her school records include this interesting comment. "Her tribe is one half degree Rogue River." Mary and Lilly would often go to Salem during the harvest season and have long visits with Rosetta, while they all worked together in the hop yards.

Eight years after Rosetta finished school, she wrote Chemawa requesting that Lillian be admitted. But for some unknown reason, Lillian did not enroll, there being no record of her attendance.

Indian Mary's youngest daughter, Lillian and friend, circa 1902.

When her schooling was finished, Rosetta returned to Grants Pass. On August 1, 1909, when she was 23, she married Alfred Farlow. They had three daughters, Mercelene, Victorine and Idora.

After Mary had lived in Grants Pass several years, she had the opportunity to visit her old friends and former canyon home.

Edith Ayer Keyte, a lifetime resident of Josephine county, and granddaughter of William Massie, who first leased Mary's ranch, tells an interesting story about Mary's visit.

"One day when my Aunt Rose was living on the Massie ranch just below present-day Indian Mary Park, she heard a knock on her front door. She was mildly surprised to find Indian Mary, her daughter Rosetta, and Rosetta's two children standing on the porch. Mary announced that she had come to pay Rose a visit.

Rose was Hal Massie's wife, one of grandfather's six sons. He was the one that found the grave of the unknown Indian.

Hiding her curiosity, and expecting the visit to be a matter of an hour or two, Rose brewed some tea and prepared to talk about old times. But Mary seemed content to listen, and smile, and nod agreement, while Rose kept the conversation going all afternoon.

When the afternoon was over and darkness approached and Mary said nothing about leaving, Rose calmly met the situation by "making down" beds on the floor for her visitors.

Rose came in for some good-natured kidding from her friends and relation, when at the end of three days, Mary abruptly announced that her visit was at an end. She solemnly shook hands and departed.

The thing that made it doubly amusing to Rose, was that Mary had never been in her home before, or ever came back again. Others that knew Mary, said that it was her way of paying a visit."

In 1920 Alfred Farlow left his family and disappeared. Rosetta signed a non-support warrant for his arrest, but the sheriff could not locate him. Rosetta supported herself and her children, working in Lempke's Grants Pass Steam Laundry.

In time, Rosetta was successful in finding her husband. He was living in Salem. She and the children moved there and the family was united. Three more children were born, Eldon, Flora and Everett.

For Mary, a parade of hurrying seasons moved across the calendar. She was quite alone, lonesome, and approaching her sunset years. She too, moved to Salem to be near her daughters and grandchildren.

It was 1922, when Lilly and a girl friend visited in Grants Pass. Local citizens were goggled-eyed and waggle-tongued, as they stared with amazement and wonder at Lilly's beautiful and expensive clothes, and her long, sleek, shiny Stutz Bearcat roadster!

Lilly told friends of her mother's death, and how she and Rosetta had honored their mother for her many years of hard work and sacrifices, keeping the family together and providing them with an education.

"We gave her a beautiful funeral", said Lilly, "that cost near $600.00 for the casket, robe, flowers and services."

Good roads and automobiles came slowly to the canyon country. Those that loved its wild solitude preferred it that way. The stage still left Merlin every other day. Along with mail, it carried groceries and supplies for the miners. At the big barn on the old "Indian ranch" the horses were changed and the driver continued his run to Almeda mine. He stayed overnight, returning the next day, with room for passengers instead of freight. About twice a month his feet rested on a battered strongbox — its secret amounts, never divulged.

Gradually, the grasping hand of change touched the last reaches of the wild river. But the stubborn Rogue retained its famous name and character, not for its heavy nuggets and Indian heritage, but for its famous fishing and wilderness beauty.

Here, the saga of Indian Mary and Umpqua Joe might have ended. But in 1958, the Josephine County Board of Commissioners bought the historic site and converted it into a beautiful public park, with facilities for swimming, camping, picnicking and travel trailers, so that the beauty of its setting and the memory of its past, could be preserved for future generations. It was named Indian Mary Park.

There is yet an epilogue.

During the summer of 1974, some special visitors came to Indian Mary Park. But theirs was more than an ordinary vacation. In the party was Everett Farlow, his wife Geraldine, his daughters Terry Boerckel and Bonnie Farlow, Terry's husband Paul, and their two children, Paul Jr. and Tannette. And what made them special?

Everett casually remarked that he was Indian Mary's grandson, and Terry and Bonnie great-granddaughters. In fact, Everett said, that it was only two years before his visit, that he had learned that a public park had been built on his grandmother's old homesite on the Rogue.

And so it was. After 118 years, the grandson stood on the very spot where Umpqua Joe built his first log cabin home.

It was then, after discussions with Everett Farlow, that it was possible to fill some of the blank spaces in the lives of Indian Mary and her children.

Everett said that Mary told his mother, that Umpqua Joe was, at one time, the chief of a band of Indians living along Grave Creek.

The family offers as proof, a copy of a treaty with the Chasta (Shasta) Indians, dated 1854, from the files of the U.S. Office of Bureau of Land Management, Portland, Oregon.

The long title of the treaty is as follows:

"Articles of a convention and agreement made and concluded at the council ground, opposite the mouth of Applegate Creek, on Rogue River, in the Territory of Oregon, on the eighteenth day of November, 1854, by Joel Palmer, superintendent of Indian Affairs, on the part of the United States, and the chiefs and head-men of the Chasta tribe of Indians, the Cow-nan-ti-co, Sa-cher-i-ton, and Na-al-ye bands of Scotons, and the Grave Creek band of Umpquas . . . "

At the end of the lengthy document is the mark of, "Little Chief, Bill, Salmon Fisher, Bushland, Sam", and lastly, "Jo, chief of the Grave Creeks".

Everett Farlow says his mother also told him that Umpqua Joe's wife was the daughter of an Umpqua chief, called, Chief George.

It seems that the tragedy of Umpqua Joe's death was to stalk the family, even to the grandchildren. Mercelene, the family believes, was murdered, but they have no knowledge of what actually happened.

Sometime during the late 1920s, Lilly fell in love with a dental student and paid his way through school. When he graduated, he showed his appreciation by mistreating her and marrying another girl. Shortly after that, Lilly disappeared and has never been seen since.

Of Mary's six grandchildren, only Everett, Eldon and Flora are living — all in Portland.

It is remembered, by the family, that Lilly received a generous amount of money, believed to have been an inheritance from Jack Fairfield, which accounted for her fine clothes and the new roadster. But the news came more than fifty years late to satisfy the curiosity of those puzzled by her grand appearance in 1922.

When Indian Mary Park was dedicated it was called, "the smallest Indian reservation in the world". Perhaps it was. But, of one thing, there is no question; the more than a hundred thousand thirsting visitors a year that are refreshed by its green peacefulness agree, that Umpqua Joe, was indeed, "a very smart man", when he picked the spot for his little log cabin home.

Not far from Salem's bustling business district, the crest of a peaceful knoll looks down on the green-clad city at its feet. There, in the pioneer City View Cemetery, is the last resting place of Mary Peters.

Cast in a bronze marker is a fitting eulogy to a native of the Canyon Country, who faced the hardships of a last frontier and earned her place among our honored pioneers.

The End

1852 MARY PETERS 1921

"INDIAN MARY" AN HONORED NATIVE DAUGHTER OF JOSEPHINE CO. OPERATED A FERRY IN THE DEEP CANYON COUNTRY OF ROGUE RIVER. HER FATHER, UMPQUA JOE, CHIEF OF THE GRAVE CREEKS, PREVENTED A MASSACRE BY WARNING EARLY DAY MINERS OF AN INDIAN ATTACK.
JOSEPHINE CO. HISTORICAL SOCIETY

Table Rock — Eternal landmark of the Rogue Valley.

ACKNOWLEDGEMENTS

The author wishes to express his gratitude to those whose help has made it possible to relive a brief page from the pioneer album of an age gone by.

INTERVIEWS

Mildred Bulter Bryce	In memoriam
Ord Crow	In memoriam
Frank Wooldridge	In memoriam
Pauline Shier	Grants Pass, Ore.
Edith Ayer Keyte	Grants Pass, Ore.
A. E. "Doc" Yarbrough	Grants Pass, Ore.
Elizabeth Hiller	Grants Pass, Ore.
Everett Farlow	Portland, Ore.
Nate Gale	Klamath Falls, Ore.

PHOTOGRAPHS

Edith Keyte	Galice ferry, Almeda mine bridge
Howard Bearss	Grants Pass-Crescent City stage
Victor Sparlin	Ira Sparlin
Josephine Co. Historical Society	Indian Mary and daughter
Ore. State Highway Travel Section	Views of Rogue canyon

DOCUMENTS — MICROFILM

Frank Walsh, historian	Grants Pass, Ore.
Betty Schoolcraft, records research	Portland, Ore.
Josephine Co. Clerk's office	Grants Pass, Ore.
Jackson Co. Clerk's office	Medford, Ore.
Southern Oregon State College	Ashland, Ore.
Jacksonville Museum	Jacksonville, Ore.
Ruth Booth, research and typing	Grants Pass, Ore.

APPENDIX

TABLE ROCK — A massive flat-topped formation of solid rock located about 8 miles northwest of Medford, Oregon. Revered by the Rogue Indians living along the river at its base, Table Rock was a symbol of strength, a self image, a guardian of their homeland.

CHIEF SAM'S VALLEY — Spreading north, east and west of Table Rock, was a flat, open valley surrounded by low foothills. In pioneer days, its growth of forage grass made it abundant in wild game. Hunters from Chief Sam's village claimed and defended it against other tribes and invading white miners and settlers. Pioneers referred to the area as Chief Sam's Valley, later shortened to Sam's Valley.

OREGON-CALIFORNIA TRAIL — Before discovery of gold in California, overland travel from the Willamette Valley through southern Oregon was limited to an occasional party of fur traders. When the great gold rush of 1849 began, early gold-seekers hacked a pack trail from the Willamette, through southern Oregon and over the Siskiyou mountains to California. So was born, the Oregon-California Trail.

CHIEFS JOHN, GEORGE AND LIMPY — When gold miners first moved into the Rogue River Valley they found Indians living in small bands, in definite areas. In general, the Rogues controlled all of the Rogue and Illinois River drainages and the upper Rogue Valley, east to the Cascade Range and south to the Siskiyou Range. The principal chiefs were Joe, Sam and Jim, chieftain brothers; along with Jake, Sambo and Tipso, all in the upper Table Rock valleys. John, Limpy and George ruled the lower Rogue and Illinois Valleys.

APPLEGATE RIVER — Named after pioneers Jesse and Lindsay Applegate. It rises in the foothills of the Siskiyou mountains and empties into the Rogue about 5 miles below Grants Pass.

TWOGOOD AND HARKNESS TAVERN — A popular stopping place on the Oregon-California Trail, located at the crossing of Grave Creek, about 24 miles north of present-day Grants Pass. James Twogood and McDonough Harkness were partners in its operation. Their roadhouse was an important "forting-up" place and center of military operations during the Rogue River Indian wars of 1855-56.

GRAVE CREEK CROSSING — An early camping spot on the Oregon-California Trail. In 1846, 14 year old Martha Leland Crowley and other members of an immigrant party, camped at the creek crossing. The young girl died of "mountain fever", (typhoid) and was buried beside the creek — hence the name Grave Creek.

JOSEPHINE CREEK — In 1851, gold was first discovered in southern Oregon on this creek. It empties into the Illinois River on the west side of Eight Dollar Mountain, a few miles northwest of Kerby, Ore. The creek was named for Josephine Rollins, who with her father and a mining party camped for several weeks near the mouth of the creek. Josephine was considered the first white woman "resident" of southern Oregon. Both the creek and Josephine County were named in her honor.

STERLING CREEK — A rich mining area about ten miles south of Jacksonville. The creek and mining town of Sterlingville were named after its discoverer.

PARAGON BAY - CRESCENT CITY — Historical accounts tell of the wrecking of the sailing vessel Paragon, swept onto off-shore rocks near present Crescent City, Calif. For a time, that portion of the coastline was known as Paragon Bay, later named Crescent City, because of the crescent shaped beach.

COW CREEK CANYON — One of a series of extremely rough and rugged canyons, comprising about 25 miles of the Oregon-California Trail between the Umpqua River and Rogue River drainages.

SCOTTSBURG — Located at the end of tidewater on the Umpqua River. Founded in 1850 by Levi Scott as a "saltwater" shipping port for small ocean vessels, to provide supplies to the miners and settlers of southern Oregon.

PRINT OF BUTTER — In pioneer days all butter was hand churned. After the butter was formed, it was packed into molds or presses, resulting in bricks of one to two pounds. The inside of these presses were often decorated with raised flowers and designs, which "printed" on the finished mold of butter—hence, a print of butter.

TARPAULIN — A type of waterproofed canvas; often shortened to "tarp". Spread atop poles, it provided a temporary shelter.

MUZZLELOADER — In pioneer days, a long barreled gun loaded with powder and shot through the barrel or muzzle.

SLUICE BOX - LONG TOMS — Sluice boxes were usually constructed in open trough fashion and fitted with "riffles". Gravel was shoveled or washed into the head of the box and the "washing" action of the flowing water, separated the heavier gold from the rock, dirt and silt, allowing it to settle behind the riffles. Long Toms were short, narrow sections of sluice boxes. When elevated at one end and water bailed onto the gravel, they provided a gold-saving, washing action, that would exceed, many times, the amount possible to pan in a day.

COLONEL JOHN C. FREMONT — In 1844, Fremont led an exploring party from Fort Vancouver, up the Columbia River to The Dalles. Then he followed Fall River, now the Deschutes, into the Klamath Lake country where he was attacked by Indians. He turned east toward Summer Lake, eventually passing into Nevada. Historians indicate that Umpqua Joe served as one of Fremont's guides on this trip.

UMPQUA TRIBE — A tribe of Indians living along the Umpqua River and Cow Creek drainages. In 1846, they were said to have numbered about 400. A count taken in 1902 on the Grand Ronde Indian reservation, tallied only 84 survivors.

DEER CREEK - ROSEBURG — Aaron Rose, a pioneer of 1851 settled at the junction of Deer Creek and the south fork of the Umpqua River. For a time the tiny settlement was known as Deer Creek, but when Rose donated land for a church and school it was named Roseburg in his honor.

SIX BIT HOUSE — Located on the Oregon-California Trail near the crossing of Wolf Creek. The original roadhouse and tavern was built about 1853, during the Rogue River Indian wars, and is frequently mentioned in pioneer history. Three drunken miners decided to hang an innocent Indian boy, "to rid the country of one of the thieving rascals". The proprietor of the house stopped the proceedings, contending that the boy owed him six bits. After the money was collected the hanging was carried out. The name Six Bit House stuck for many years.

INDIAN GRAPEVINE — News and battle plans were often carried by Indian runners from one village or tribe to another. It was referred to by the whites as "Indian grapevine".

CAPTAIN ANDREW JACKSON SMITH — Commander of Fort Lane. Established in 1853, it was the only regular army post in southern Oregon. It was located on the south side of Rogue River at Table Rock, across the river from the Indian reservation. His command consisted of three companies of dragoons and one of infantry.

DRAGOONS — A term used by the U.S. Army, in the 1850s, to designate mounted infantry. Dragoons were armed with special short barreled versions of the regular army musket. It was more adaptable to use by mounted men, but its range and accuracy were poor.

INDIAN SIGN — A broad reference to many things used in tracking and locating eluding war parties. Tracks, broken twigs and turned rocks; such things as entrails of game animals, feathers from game birds, fish cleanings, and berries picked from bushes — all were "Indian sign" — indicating a party had passed — and how long ago.

FLAMING ARROWS — The Rogues knew the advantages of being able to set fires at a distance with flaming arrows. The most common type was to lash tinder-dry grass to an arrow shaft, which was lighted and launched immediately. Hotter burning, longer lasting arrows were smeared with pitch from pine trees.

WAR FEATHERS — Contrary to popular conceptions, Rogue warriors did not go into combat dressed in feather bonnets and war robes. Actually they stripped to the barest amount of clothing necessary for warmth and protection — belts to carry weapons, and quivers for arrows. They smeared their naked bodies with colored orchers and clays, often displaying their war status with a single white feather in their headband.

SHASTA - CHASTA — Early studies indicate that at one time the Shasta Indians extended from the mid Klamath River area of northern California, over the Siskiyou mountains, and included the entire valley of Stuart Creek (now Bear Creek) and Butte Creek in the upper Rogue Valley. Closely allied with the Shastas were the Takelmas, (commonly referred to as Rogues) who inhabited the lower Rogue drainages, including the Illinois and Applegate Valleys, and the areas of lower Grave Creek, Jump-off Joe, Louse and Galice Creeks. Early treaties of the U.S. Government with these tribes, usually referred to them as "Chastas".

PUNCHEON FLOOR — Log cabins of the earliest miners and settlers usually had dirt floors. One of the first improvements was a puncheon floor. Straight poles were cut and their sides hewed to fit tightly together. They were laid directly on the dirt. After the tops were hewed flat with a hand adz and dirt had filled the cracks, the floor was tight, warm and reasonably smooth.

COLONEL JOHN E. ROSS — John Ross of Jacksonville assumed command of the Ninth Regiment of the Oregon Territorial Militia in 1855. Ross's command was comprised mainly of volunteers from the mines and settlements of the Rogue and Illinois Valley. The volunteers, as they were always called, operated on their own initiative under their own officers but in liaison with U.S. Army troops.

GEORGE LAW CURRY — Curry was governor of Oregon Territory in 1853. A newspaper man, he had been editor of Oregon's first paper, the Oregon City Spectator. Curry county is named in his honor.

FORT LELAND — In the fall of 1855, volunteer troops established a camp at the Grave Creek crossing, calling it Fort Leland. It provided a headquarters camp for patrols along the trail through Cow Creek canyon and for operations in the canyon country of the lower Rogue. The name Leland honored Martha Leland Crowley who was buried beside the creek in 1846, and was the first white woman to die in the Rogue Country.

MULE CREEK — A tributary of Rogue River, located in the extreme northeast corner of Curry county and empties into the Rogue about 35 miles below Galice. In 1852 a party of soldiers stationed at Fort Orford on the coast, were attempting to make their way through the wild canyon country to aid Indian threatened settlers in the Rogue Valley. While camped beside a creek a pack mule named John, strayed and was lost. The creek became known as John Mule Creek and was so marked on early-day maps, later shortened to Mule Creek.

BIG MEADOWS — A high-ridge meadow land of several hundred acres on the north side of the Rogue in the Mule Creek area The meadows were abundant in lush "prairie" grass, affording unlimited forage for pack mules and horses, an absolute necessity to the volunteer forces in carrying out the last phase of the Indian wars of 1855-56.

FERRY OPERATIONS — Ferries on the Rogue were built of heavy planks, flat-bottomed and square-ended. A windlass, or lever system was used to raise and lower platforms at each end, so that passengers or teams could move from the ferry to the "landing". They were current operated; a cable being strung from bank to bank and anchored to sturdy trees. The ferry was attached to the cable by means of a pulley and cable system. After being poled away from the bank, the ferry was pushed across the river by its natural current.

LEE JACK — The news of the discovery of gold in California and the rush that followed quickly spread all over the world. Thousands of Chinese coolies bonded themselves at exorbitant interest rates to rich Chinese land owners for passage expenses to the California mines. Many drifted north to Oregon. Being aliens, they were not legally allowed to file gold claims. They were tolerated, mainly because they provided a cheap labor pool for stage road and railroad construction. They had great patience and would mine lean ground and work at tasks ordinary miners shunned. As did most frontier towns, Grants Pass in its golden days had its share of Chinese cooks and laundries.

GRANTS PASS — Named in honor of Gen. U. S. Grant. The little town grew along the railroad right of way after the Oregon and California Railroad Company laid track through the Rogue Valley in

December, 1883. Prior to that time it was only a stage stop on the Oregon-California road, near the present north I-5 interchange.

MERLIN — During railroad construction in the Rogue Valley, an end of track headquarters was established a few miles northwest of Grants Pass which eventually became Merlin. A postoffice was established in 1886, and for a time was called McCallister, later changed to Merlin. It is said that a railroad construction engineer suggested the name Merlin, because of birds in the area which he believed were merlins, a member of the falcon family.

PHEMORAL ARTERY - FEMORAL — A great artery in the thigh.

DR. FRANK L. VAN DYKE — One of the first doctors to locate in Grants Pass, in 1883. He was elected first mayor of Grants Pass, serving one term during 1887 and 1888.

PROF. H. L. BENSON — Henry L. Benson was the third principal (1886 to 1892) of the Grants Pass public school system. He was a much respected educator and a popular leader in civic affairs. Early day schools were called academies.

WALDO — An early mining community in southern Josephine county. The rough, little gold town became the first county seat of Josephine county in January, 1856. There was much uncertainty of the location of the boundary line between Oregon and California. Most miners in the area believed their claims were in California and supported California politicians. In 1853 William Waldo was nominated for Governor of California. Because Waldo had performed favors for the miners, they named the mining village in his honor.

CLUSTER LIGHTS — In 1910, Grants Pass proudly called itself "The City of Lights" after installing its first "modern" street lights — three to a block. Ten foot cast iron posts were topped with a "cluster" of three round, white globes. A city ordinance was immediately passed, making it unlawful to tie horses or teams to the new lights.

AMOS E. VOORHIES — Pioneer Grants Pass newspaper publisher. He began publishing the Rogue River Weekly Courier in 1897. To Mr. Voorhies goes much of the credit for preserving the history of Grants Pass and Josephine county.

STUTZ BEARCAT — An expensive roadster built in the 1920s. It was considered the ultimate in class and style for its time. Depending upon options, its cost ranged from three to six thousand dollars.

Guardian of the Rogue River Valley, southern anchor of the Cascades — Snowy Butte. Rogue Valley pioneers admired the snow-crested peak and liked the name, Snowy Butte. But each generation had its preference and the often-named mountain has been called, Big Butte, Jackson Peak, John Quincy Adams, Mt. Pitt and finally, Mt. McLoughlin. Regardless of name, the imposing landmark has remained a monument of beauty — an inspiration of renewed courage and strength — for more than a hundred years of travelers, making their way through the Valleys of the Rogue.